12/07

ENERGY FOR THE FUTURE AND GLOBAL WARMING

HYDROGEN FUEL

By Andrew Solway

Consultant: Suzy Gazlay, M.A.,
science curriculum resource teacher

Gareth Stevens
Publishing

Please visit our web site at: www.garethstevens.com
For a free color catalog describing Gareth Stevens Publishing's
list of high-quality books, call 1-800-542-2595 (USA) or
1-800-387-3178 (Canada).

Library of Congress Cataloging-in-Publication Data

Solway, Andrew.
    Hydrogen fuel / Andrew Solway.
        p. cm. — (Energy for the future and global warming)
    Includes index.
    ISBN: 978-0-8368-8401-2 (lib. bdg.)
    ISBN: 978-0-8368-8410-4 (softcover)
    1. Hydrogen as fuel—Juvenile literature. I. Title.
TP359.H8.S65   2008
665.8'1—dc22   2007008751

This edition first published in 2008 by
Gareth Stevens Publishing
A Weekly Reader® Company
1 Reader's Digest Road
Pleasantville, NY 10570-7000 USA

Copyright © 2008 by Gareth Stevens, Inc.

Produced by Discovery Books
Editors: Geoff Barker and Sabrina Crewe
Designer: Keith Williams
Photo researchers: Sabrina Crewe and Rachel Tisdale
Illustrations: Stefan Chabluk

Gareth Stevens editor: Carol Ryback
Gareth Stevens art direction: Tammy West
Gareth Stevens production: Jessica Yanke

Photo credits: PAC-Car II—ETH Zurich: cover; title page; 21. NASA:
/ A. Caulet St-ECF/ESA 5; / James McDivitt 20. U.S. Fish & Wildlife Service: 8.
Getty Images / Hulton Archive: 11. Ballard Power Systems: 16. Courtesy of
U.S. Army: 22. DaimlerChrysler, Project: Fuel Cell Buses: 24. Toyota Motor Europe
S.A./N.V.: 27. Jadoo / National Hydrogen Association: 28. Engineering and Physical
Sciences Research Council: 29.

Printed in the United States of America

1 2 3 4 5 6 7 8 9 11 10 09 08 07

CONTENTS

Cover photo: For the equivalent of about two gallons (7.6 liters) of gasoline, the PAC–Car II could make a trip around the world!

Words in **boldface** appear in the glossary or in the "Key Words" boxes within the chapters.

CHAPTER ONE

ENERGY AND GLOBAL WARMING

How much energy do you need each day? A wild animal can survive on just the food it eats. Animals use food for energy. People also need food to provide energy for their bodies. But they use many other kinds of other energy in their daily lives.

People use energy to light buildings and keep them warm or cool. We need energy to grow food and to get it to stores. Then we use more energy to cook the food. We use energy for transportation and to power all kinds of machines.

Energy for the future

Today, the world gets more than 85 percent of its energy from oil, coal, and natural gas. We call these **fossil fuels**. They are fuels that formed from plants and animals that lived long ago. We burn fossil fuels to make energy.

The world's supply of fossil fuels will not last forever. Every year, we use 1 to 2 percent more energy than the year before. By 2050, we will be using more than twice as much energy as in 2000. The populations of countries around the world are growing fast. These countries are building new industries, too. Their energy needs are growing.

Running out of energy

A few countries have large amounts of fossil fuels. Many

HYDROGEN: THE WONDER FUEL

- Hydrogen is the simplest element (basic substance).
- Hydrogen is also the first known element. Scientists believe it formed soon after the universe began.
- Hydrogen is the most abundant substance in the universe.
- Hydrogen powers the Sun and all the stars. Huge clouds of hydrogen gas also float freely in space.
- Hydrogen is part of many substances found on Earth.
- Hydrogen has more energy per weight than any other fuel.

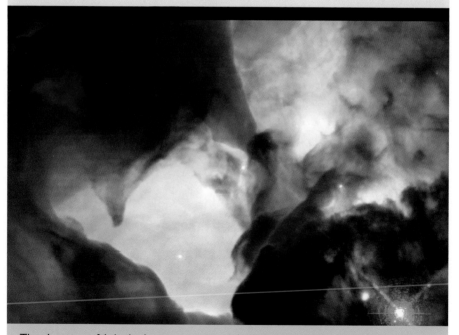

The Lagoon Nebula in outer space is an enormous cloud of gases and dust far from Earth. It is seventy times bigger than the entire solar system. The green areas above are hydrogen gas.

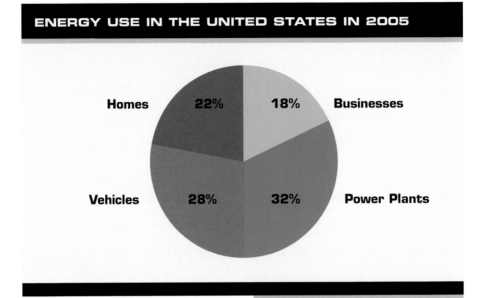

ENERGY USE IN THE UNITED STATES IN 2005

Homes 22%

18% Businesses

Vehicles 28%

32% Power Plants

This chart shows energy use in the United States. It shows how much was used by homes, businesses, power plants, and all types of vehicles.

countries must buy the fossil fuels they need. Some fossil fuel supplies might be used up sooner than expected. The faster we use up the supply of fossil fuels, the faster prices for them will rise. Some countries may soon be unable to afford enough fuel.

Global pollution

When we burn fossil fuels, such as coal, oil, and natural gas, they give off smoke and gases. These gases **pollute** our planet. They make the air, water, and land dirty.

Smog is one kind of air pollution. Gases from vehicles cause this thick, dirty fog to form. Smog can cause health problems. Most big cities get smog, especially in warm weather. The wastes that go into the air when fossil fuels burn also causes

HYDROGEN FUEL

GOOD THINGS	PROBLEMS
Renewable	Can be expensive to produce
Clean	Producing hydrogen fuel uses up fossil fuels
Can be produced in large and small amounts	Harder to store than some other fuels
Can be made anywhere	Can be difficult to transport
Produces much more energy than fossil fuels when burned	Needs careful handling
Great possibilities for the future	Everyday use will require huge changes in vehicle design

acid rain, sleet, or snow. This pollution kills fish in lakes and rivers. It harms trees, other plants, and buildings.

We have ways to stop pollution. Waste gases from vehicles are cleaned before they get into the air. **Power plants** are changing, too. Power plants usually burn fossil fuels to make energy for our homes. Some power plants are cutting the amount of pollution they produce. But we must find more ways to cut smog and acid rain.

Global effects

Fossil fuel burning releases **carbon dioxide** and other "greenhouse gases" into the air. Greenhouse gases trap Earth's heat energy. The amounts of greenhouse gases

GLOBAL WARMING

Global warming affects the whole Earth. The polar ice caps are large areas of ice at the North Pole and South Pole. The ice caps are melting more than usual. The extra melting changes the lives of people and animals that live in those areas.

Global warming is also slowly turning parts of the world into desert. In some places, farmers are having trouble growing food crops. Each year, more hurricanes and other extreme types of weather occur. Forest fires are getting more common. The rate of global warming will keep rising for at least another fifty years.

Polar bears and other animals need lots of ice in their Arctic habitat. If ice in polar regions continues to melt at greater rates, many animals will suffer.

PROBLEMS FOR THE FUTURE

Our increasing use of fossil fuels puts more greenhouse gases into the air every year. This makes global warming happen faster. If we cut down on the amount of fossil fuels burned, we will reduce the amount of greenhouse gases in the air. The use of renewable fuels will help us achieve this goal.

in the air have increased in the last one hundred years. High levels of greenhouse gases cause Earth to get warmer. This changes the worldwide weather patterns, or climate. The climate change is called **global warming**.

To stop or slow global warming, we need to release fewer waste gases. One way to do this is to burn fewer fossil fuels. Another way is to use fuels that are **renewable**. A renewable source of energy does not run out.

We are testing different kinds of renewable fuels. Some of these will power our vehicles and others will help produce electricity.

One kind of renewable energy that can replace fossil fuels is hydrogen gas. It is rich in energy. Hydrogen gas is an exciting future fuel.

KEY WORDS

gas: a substance with no fixed shape, like oxygen or hydrogen. Gas is sometimes a mix of other gases, like the air around us.
global warming: the gradual warming of Earth's climate
renewable: having a new or reusable supply of material constantly available

CHAPTER TWO

MAKING THE WONDER FUEL

So what is hydrogen? Why is it a good fuel? Where can we find it?

Lighter than air

Hydrogen is a very light gas. It is the lightest substance known. Hydrogen gas is very common in space. On Earth, it is mixed in other things, such as water. If we want to use hydrogen for energy, we have to produce it from substances that contain the gas.

Hydrogen combines with oxygen from the air to form water. It also combines with an element called **carbon**. (An element is a basic, pure substance.)

Hydrogen and carbon combine to form many different substances. Plants can combine carbon and hydrogen to make food. Fossil fuels are combinations of hydrogen and carbon.

Is it safe?

Hydrogen burns easily. If it did not, it would be no good as a fuel! Because it is **flammable** (easily burned),

" . . . Yes, my friends, I believe that water will one day be employed as fuel, that hydrogen and oxygen . . . will furnish an inexhaustible source of heat and light. . . . Water will be the coal of the future."

—Jules Verne, author,
The Mysterious Island (1874)

EXPLOSION

Hydrogen was used to fill airships because it is so light. The airship *Hindenburg* was filled with hydrogen gas. On May 6, 1937, it burst into flames while landing in Lakehurst, New Jersey. The hydrogen gas that filled the airship was part of the reason it burned. A coating on the outside of the *Hindenburg* made it burn extra fiercely. Helium gas replaced hydrogen in airships that were built after the *Hindenburg* disaster. Helium is not flammable.

The *Hindenburg* was 804 feet (245 meters) long — longer than three Boeing 747 jumbo jets. The airship exploded as it was landing.

HYDROGEN TODAY

About 50 million tons (45 million tonnes) of hydrogen is made globally every year. The United States makes about 9 million tons (8.2 million tonnes). That is enough hydrogen to fuel 20 to 30 million cars. Most of the hydrogen made today is used by industries. About two-thirds of the hydrogen produced by the United States is used in the ammonia industry. Ammonia is a chemical used in fertilizers.

hydrogen must be stored and used carefully.

Hydrogen fuel is not easy to store because it is a gas. It must be compressed (squeezed) and stored in a tightly closed container.

Burning hydrogen

Hydrogen produces a large amount of energy when it burns. It makes about three times as much energy as gasoline. Even better, it makes no carbon dioxide or pollutants when it burns. It only produces water.

Two ways of using hydrogen

We can burn hydrogen as a fuel for vehicle engines. An even better way to use hydrogen is to power **fuel cells**. A fuel cell is a device that makes electricity. We can use fuels cells for many purposes. Why don't we use more hydrogen fuel cells?

The problem is not with the fuel cells themselves. The

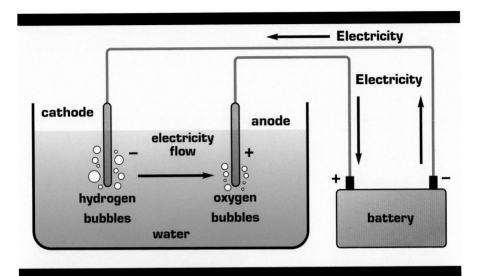

Electrolysis means "breaking apart with electricity." We use electrolysis to separate water into hydrogen and oxygen gases. Electricity from the battery passes through the water. The hydrogen gas separates from the water. It forms bubbles around the negative **electrode**. The hydrogen gas bubbles can be collected and used for power.

problem is finding a good source of hydrogen. Most of the hydrogen we use is produced from natural gas. Hydrogen made this way is cheap. But natural gas is not renewable. It is a fossil fuel. We need a different way of producing hydrogen to power fuel cells.

Making hydrogen with electricity

When hydrogen burns, it combines with oxygen to make water. We can make hydrogen by reversing this process. We use electricity to do this. The method is called electrolysis. The electricity splits the water into hydrogen and oxygen gases. There is a problem with making hydrogen this way.

PHOTOSYNTHESIS

Plants produce energy by photosynthesis — using sunlight to grow. Most leaves contain plant cells called chloroplasts. They are the green plant cells that trap the Sun's energy. Some of that energy helps split water into hydrogen and oxygen. The leaves give off oxygen to the air. A plant also takes in carbon dixoide from the air. It combines the hydrogen with carbon dioxide to grow taller and produce more leaves. In this way, plants make their own food using the Sun's energy.

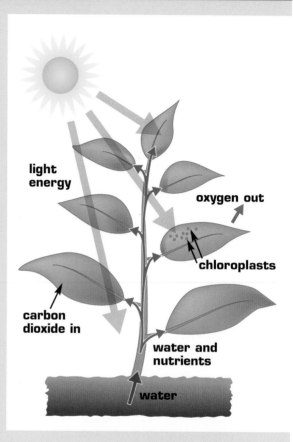

light energy

oxygen out

chloroplasts

carbon dioxide in

water and nutrients

water

It takes a lot of electricity to make electrolysis occur. This electricity is produced using other fuel sources. So, using electrolysis to make hydrogen ends up costing a lot more than using almost any other kind of fuel!

Making hydrogen from light

Most green plants use the energy in sunlight to produce their own food. This is called **photosynthesis.**

In photosynthesis, plants produce food, not hydrogen. Some very simple plant-like organisms (living things) called **algae** do produce hydrogen, however.

Pond power

Algae can grow in freshwater or saltwater. One kind of algae that produces hydrogen is often called "pond scum." It forms the green layer you see on the surface of ponds.

Algae usually produce tiny amounts of hydrogen. But U.S. scientists discovered a way to make algae produce more hydrogen than normal. They did this by changing the chemicals in the water.

Maybe one day, we will run our cars on pond scum! Now, however, hydrogen produced by algae is not cheap enough for everyday use. Scientists are working to grow algae that produce more hydrogen.

Other scientists are also hoping to find different ways of producing large amounts of hydrogen easily and cheaply for the future.

KEY WORDS

carbon: a common element (basic substance) found in all living or once-living organisms, including plants, people, animals, and all fossil fuels

electrolysis: using electricity to break down substances into their basic elements

flammable: easily burned

photosynthesis: the process by which plants use the enery in sunlight to grow

CHAPTER THREE

ALL ABOUT FUEL CELLS

Something that is efficient works well and doesn't waste energy. Hydrogen fuel cells are very efficient. They are quiet and

Fuel cells are more efficient than ordinary engines. Right now, however, fuel cells cost a lot more to make. The fuel cell below is as powerful as a 2.0-liter car engine. You can get an idea of the size of this fuel cell by comparing it to the pen and clipboard.

reliable. Fuel cells do not produce carbon dioxide or other polluting chemicals.

Engines that burn hydrogen fuel or fossil fuels cannot turn all of that fuel's energy into power. Some fuel is wasted in the burning process. Using a fuel cell is different. It makes electricity from the hydrogen instead of burning it as fuel. Electric power made this way is an efficient form of energy.

What is a fuel cell?

A fuel cell is similar to a battery. It produces electricity from **chemical reactions** (changes caused by chemicals mixing). Most batteries are used up when the chemicals inside them run out.

INSIDE AN ATOM

A cluster called the nucleus is at the center of an atom. The nucleus usually contains tiny parts called neutrons and protons. Protons have a positive (+) electric charge. Neutrons have no charge. Even smaller parts called electrons zip around the nucleus. Electrons have a negative (-) charge. The opposite charges attract one another. Hydrogen atoms are very simple. They have one proton, one electron, and no neutrons.

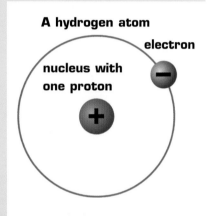

A hydrogen atom

electron

nucleus with one proton

A hydrogen atom consists of one proton (+) and one electron (-).

The chemicals in a fuel cell don't get used up. They come from a separate fuel tank. As long as there is fuel in the tank, the fuel cell keeps running. Today, most fuel cells use hydrogen for fuel.

How does a fuel cell work?
In a fuel cell, hydrogen combines with oxygen from the air to make water. This is the same chemical reaction that happens when hydrogen burns. In a fuel cell, the reaction makes electricity.

A hydrogen atom has only one proton and one electron. To make electricity, the proton and electron need to be split apart. A fuel cell can do this.

Each side of the fuel cell has a metal bar called an electrode. The electrodes are like the positive and negative poles of a battery. They form a loop, or **circuit**. The circuit carries an electrical current.

Electrons split off (1) and travel through the circuit (2) to make electricity. Protons travel to the cathode. Hydrogen reforms and unites with oxygen. Water vapor (3) and heat (4) are produced.

Splitting the hydrogen

Hydrogen comes in on one side of the fuel cell. Electrons in the hydrogen are attracted to the positive electrode. It is called the anode. The electrons split away from the protons. The electrons travel through the electrical circuit. On the way, they produce electricity. The electrons keep

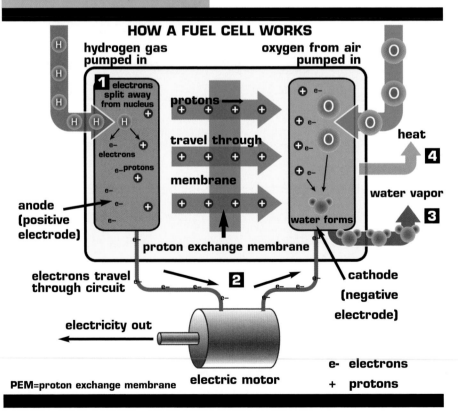

HOW A FUEL CELL WORKS

hydrogen gas pumped in

oxygen from air pumped in

1 electrons split away from nucleus

protons →

travel through

membrane

electrons

e- protons

anode (positive electrode)

proton exchange membrane

heat **4**

water vapor **3**

water forms

cathode (negative electrode)

electrons travel through circuit **2**

electricity out

electric motor

PEM=proton exchange membrane

e- electrons

+ protons

going through the circuit. They end up on the other side of the fuel cell.

On the other side of the cell

Meanwhile, what happens to the protons? They will pass through a sheet of plastic in the middle of the fuel cell. The plastic is called a proton exchange membrane (PEM).

The protons move toward the negative electrode, or cathode, on the other side of the PEM. Only the protons can pass through the PEM. Once through, the protons meet up with the electrons that came through the circuit. They join to form hydrogen atoms again.

Oxygen is pumped into the side of the fuel cell near the cathode. The hydrogen atoms combine with the

oxygen to make water. (Water has two hydrogen atoms and one oxygen atom.)

Using the fuel cell's power

The flow of electrons through the circuit creates an electric current. Flowing electrons make electricity.

As the current flows, we can use the electricity to do work. The current can light a lightbulb or power an electric motor.

We can use the electricity produced by fuel cells in many ways.

KEY WORDS

circuit: a closed loop that forms a path for an electrical current
electrode: a part of an electrical circuit that conducts electricity
fuel cell: a device that makes electricity from fuel

CHAPTER FOUR

USING HYDROGEN FUEL CELLS

Early fuel cells were not very powerful. In 1983, Canadian engineer Geoffrey Ballard began working to improve them. By 1992, his fuel cells were producing ten times more power than earlier ones. Long before that, astronauts used fuel cells in space.

British engineer Francis T. Bacon designed the first practical fuel cells. A version of these fuel cells produced electricity and water for Gemini and Apollo spacecraft in the 1960s. Fuel cells are also used aboard the space shuttles. In 1965, Edward H. White made the first space walk by an American astronaut. Here, White floats from the hatch of his *Gemini 4* spacecraft.

PAC-Car II is powered by a small hydrogen fuel cell. It produces no pollution. PAC-Car II is tiny and very light. Only one person can fit inside it. The car weighs about the same as two mountain bikes. The PAC-Car II is very efficient. It can travel for 15,275 miles (24,583 kilometers) using only about 1 gallon (3.8 liters) of gasoline! Right now, the PAC-Car II is not a practical car. It is still in the testing stages. But it gives us an idea of what cars of the future might be like.

The PAC-Car II is so efficient, it could drive all the way around the world on only about 2 gallons (7.6 l) of gasoline!

New cars

In the late 1990s, many carmakers built **experimental** cars powered by fuel cells.

Fuel cells are great for vehicles because they produce clean energy. Cars and trucks are major producers of pollution.

Hydrogen is a clean fuel. It does not produce pollution.

Fuel cell cars are still very new and expensive. For this reason, there are not many on the road yet. Fuel cell vehicles are reliable, however. They will last as long as cars that run on gasoline. Fuel cell vehicles perform as well as gasoline-powered vehicles.

Fuel cell cars need heavy fuel tanks to store their compressed hydrogen fuel. Fuel tanks are improving,

In September 2006, the U.S. Army began testing this vehicle on army bases. It is the Chevrolet Equinox, a fuel cell car. These cars will be tested in cities, too.

". . . We are at the **peak** of the oil age and at the same time the beginning of the hydrogen age. . . . The long-term future will be in hydrogen and fuel cells."

Herman Kuipers, **innovation** & research manager, Shell Oil, Amsterdam, The Netherlands, 2000

however. Hydrogen cars sold today can travel about 350 miles (563 km) on one tank of fuel.

More hydrogen vehicles

People are starting to use more hydrogen-powered vehicles. Some of the vehicles burn hydrogen as fuel for their engines. Others use hydrogen fuel cells that make electricity for the cars.

The U.S. Army and several U.S. police forces are testing hydrogen-powered cars. Canada is developing the "Hydrogen Highway" for the 2010 Winter Olympic Games in Whistler, Canada.

Hydrogen power is being used for larger vehicles, too. Chicago, Illinois, tested some hydrogen-fueled buses and asked riders what they thought. Most riders liked the hydrogen-fueled buses.

Setting goals

People are becoming more aware of global warming. They are also concerned that fossil fuels will become more scarce and expensive. In the United States, the government has set goals to increase hydrogen use in the coming years. Across the nation, people are ready to **invest** in (put time and money into) new forms of energy for the future. Hydrogen is one of these future fuel sources.

KEY WORDS

experimental: having to do with an experiment (testing something new to see if it works)
innovation: a new idea or method
invest: to put in time or money
peak: the highest point; at its strongest

CHAPTER FIVE

HYDROGEN FOR THE FUTURE

We will need to make a lot of changes to switch to using hydrogen as a fuel. It involves more than changing to fuel-cell cars. How will cars and other vehicles get the hydrogen they need? We will have to build new filling stations.

We will also need to build factories that make hydrogen from water. Power plants

". . . Hydrogen can fill critical energy needs beyond transportation. Hydrogen can also be used to heat and generate electricity for our homes. The future possibilities of this energy source are enormous."

U.S. Congressman Dan Lipinski, 2006 (Democrat–Illinois)

A hydrogen filling station stores the fuel as liquid hydrogen in tanks. The hydrogen must be turned into a gas before being used in vehicles.

PROBLEM SOLVED?

In 2006, chemists Don Gervasio and Sonja Tasic at Arizona State University in Tempe, Arizona, found a new way to store and release hydrogen. They dissolved the chemical borohydride in water. They found the liquid could store a lot of hydrogen. Hydrogen stored this way does not have to be cooled or compressed (squeezed). The hydrogen can also be easily released for use. Their discovery may lead the way to smaller, cheaper, and longer-lasting fuel cells. These handy fuel cells could provide power for cameras, laptops, and other electronic devices.

that supply our homes with electricity will need to switch fuels, too. It will be a huge job for power plants to switch from using **generators** that burn fossil fuels.

We will not be able to use our oil pipelines to transport hydrogen. Hydrogen gas can escape through the tiniest hole in a container. Instead, we will need tankers (huge ships with large tanks) and pipelines that are airtight.

A high price

We must do all we can to slow global warming. One way is to cut **emissions** (wastes produced by fuels).

Fuel cells for cars and power plants are expensive, however. It will cost a lot of money to change to vehicles and power plants that can handle hydrogen. We cannot switch over to hydrogen power until it is cheap enough for everyday use.

Looking ahead

It is always cheaper to produce large quantities of a product. So, the more we use hydrogen for fuel, the faster the cost will drop. At first, we may use hydrogen mixed with natural gas. This mixture produces almost no pollution. Using this mix in engines and power plants will help reduce global warming.

The cheaper fuel cells get, the more they will be used. We will use fuel cells in trucks, boats, and even aircraft. Hospitals might use a fuel cell generator for backup electricity in case of a power failure.

Buildings that use fuel cells for power will get two benefits. The fuels cells will provide electricity. These

GOAL: ZERO EMISSIONS

Iceland has a goal. It plans to cut its carbon dioxide emissions to zero by 2050. Iceland has already begun working toward changing the kinds of fuels it uses. Because of its location, Iceland uses plenty of geothermal energy (natural heat from Earth stored underground as hot water and steam). Nearly every home there is heated by geothermal energy. Most of Iceland's vehicles still run on oil, however. But Iceland is now starting to use hydrogen-powered buses. Hydrogen for these buses is produced from water and electricity. The electricity is made without using fossil fuels. The hydrogen used to power Iceland's vehicles is truly clean energy. Iceland may well reach its goal!

fuel cell stack

This is a cutaway of a hybrid car, the Toyota Prius. The Prius has a gasoline engine and can also run on an electric motor.

buildings will also be warmed by heat produced by the fuel cells.

The Honda Motor Company is developing and testing cars powered by a fuel cell stack (a group of fuel cells).

The fuel cell stack will do two jobs at once. It will make enough hydrogen fuel to power a fuel-cell car. It will also produce enough extra heat to warm a house.

A hydrogen future

Fifty years from now, we should be able to make hydrogen cheaply from water. Hydrogen may then become our main energy source. All the hydrogen power we use will produce only one kind of **waste** — water. The water can be used or released into the air as water vapor. In the air, it will form clouds and later fall as rain. The rain will run into rivers and lakes. The water can be reused to make more hydrogen for fuel.

Hydrogen fuel's future

Hydrogen fuel cells will play an important part in our future energy needs. The energy to make hydrogen will come from several sources. At first, we may need to use fossil fuels to make hydrogen. Where possible, we will use wind energy, solar (Sun) energy, or other clean sources. We may also have "hydrogen farms" where farmers will make hydrogen from algae.

As our energy needs grow, we will learn to make clean energy. We will use energy more efficiently. Hydrogen fuel will help us.

This video camera runs on a hydrogen fuel cell. Fuel cells could soon be used for laptops, cell phones, and other electronic equipment. A laptop computer powered by a fuel cell could work for ten hours before it needs more fuel.

KEY WORDS

bacteria: microscopic, one-celled life forms

emission: a substance, such as carbon dioxide, that is given off by burning coal, oil, or some other fuel

generator: a machine that turns mechanical energy into electrical energy

waste: an unusable product that can sometimes pollute the air, land, or water

CANDY POWER

A 2006 experiment at the University of Birmingham, in England, showed a new way to make hydrogen. Professor Lynne Macaskie and her team got leftover caramel and other candy from a candy factory. They put it in a drum (top). They added **bacteria** (tiny life forms with only one cell) that like to munch on sugar. When the bacteria ate the candy, they gave off hydrogen. The hydrogen passed into a fuel cell (bottom) that powered a little fan. The team had developed a new, clean way to make hydrogen. This discovery used up leftovers that would otherwise become trash. Less waste, more clean energy—the wonder fuel at work!

drum

fuel cell

fan

GLOSSARY

algae: usually tiny, plant-like life forms that live in water

carbon dioxide: a gas given off by decaying plants and by the burning of fuels. Plants use it to make food. Too much carbon dioxide in the air worsens global warming.

chemical reaction: the mixing of two or more substances to make new substances

circuit: a closed loop that forms a path for an electric current

electrode: a part of an electric circuit that helps conduct electricity

emission: a waste substance given off, usually when some type of fuel is burned

fossil fuels: fuels, including coal, oil, and natural gas, that formed in the ground from living matter over millions of years

fuel cell: a device that makes electricity from fuel

generator: a machine that turns mechanical energy into electrical energy

global warming: the gradual warming of Earth's climate

innovation: a new and usually improved idea or method

pollute: to make land, air, or water dirty

power plant: a factory that produces electricity

renewable: having a new or reusable supply of material constantly available

The following list highlights the major fuel sources of the twenty-first century. It also lists some advantages and disadvantages of each.

	Advantages	Disadvantages
Biofuels	renewable energy source; widely available from a number of sources, including farms, restaurants, and everday garbage	fossil fuels often used to grow farm crops; requires special processing facilities that run on fossil fuels in order to produce usable biofuel
Fossil fuels: coal, oil, petroleum	used by functioning power plants worldwide; supports economies	limited supplies; emit greenhouse gases; produce toxic wastes; must often be transported long distances
Geothermal energy	nonpolluting; renewable; free source	only available in localized areas; would require redesign of heating systems
Hydrogen (fuel cells)	most abundant element in the universe; nonpolluting	production uses up fossil fuels; storage presents safety issues
Nuclear energy	produces no greenhouse gases; produces a lot of energy from small amounts of fuel	solid wastes remain dangerous for centuries; limited life span of power plants
Solar power	renewable; produces no pollutants; free source	weather and climate dependent; solar cells expensive to manufacture
Water power	renewable resource; generally requires no additional fuel	requires flowing water, waves, or tides; can interfere with view; dams may destroy large natural areas and disrupt human settlements
Wind power	renewable; nonpolluting; free source	depends on weather patterns; depends on location; endangers bird populations

RESOURCES

Books

Tocci, Salvatore.
Hydrogen and Noble Gases.
True Books (series).
Children's Press (2004).

Walker, Niki.
Hydrogen: Running on Water.
Energy Revolution (series).
Crabtree (2007).

Web Sites

www.eia.doe.gov/kids/energyfacts/sources/IntermediateHydrogen.html
Explore the United States' Department of Energy Web site regarding the use of hydrogen as an energy source.

http://inventors.about.com/od/fstartinventions/a/Fuel_Cells.htm
Learn about the development of the fuel cell.

Publisher's note to educators and parents: Our editors have carefully reviewed these Web sites to ensure that they are suitable for children. Many Web sites change frequently, however, and we cannot guarantee that a site's future contents will continue to meet our high standards of quality and educational value. Be advised that children should be closely supervised whenever they access the Internet.

INDEX